Data and Information for Executive Decisions in Higher Education

About the Author

Dennis P. Jones—As Director of Information Standards and Studies at NCHEMS in the seventies, oversaw the development and adoption of standard definitions and organizing principles for the collection, reporting, and exchange of information in postsecondary-education . . . Associate Director of NCHEMS for Planning and Evaluation since 1980 . . . 1961-1969, analyst in Planning Office and Business Office, Rensselaer Polytechnic Institute . . . M.S. in Management Engineering from R.P.I., with concentration in statistics and operations research . . . coauthor of *State-Level Information Base*, *Higher Education Facilities Planning and Management Manuals* . . . author of numerous professional papers . . . frequent consultant to U.S. Office of Education, National Center for Education Statistics, National Science Foundation, and numerous colleges and universities and state-level higher-education agencies.

An NCHEMS Executive Overview

Data and Information for Executive Decisions in Higher Education

Dennis P. Jones

1982

National Center for Higher Education Management Systems
P.O. Drawer P   Boulder, Colorado 80302
An Affirmative Action / Equal Opportunity Employer

Contents

CHAPTER 1

Introduction

This has been called the postindustrial era, in which there has emerged an "information society," as sociologist Daniel Bell terms it. The U.S. Department of Commerce published statistics in 1980 showing that the so-called information industries now employ half the national work force and account for half the gross national product. This helps confirm Bell's observation that "exchange of information in terms of various kinds of data processing, record keeping, market research and so forth is the foundation for most economic exchanges. Data-transmission systems are the transforming resource of the society...information and knowledge frame the problems of a post-industrial society" (1976, p. 46).

Even in higher education, where organizational life is more than ordinarily resistant to change, the new data-processing and communications technology has permanently intruded upon the cloister. Reporting and exchange of data are already the predominant forms of communication among institutions of higher education and between the institutions and their constituencies. Several studies in recent years have shown that either by choice or by necessity, most American colleges and universities are investing heavily in the creation and maintenance of data resources—and expect to continue to do so.

Dennis P. Jones

By and large, that investment has yet to pay large dividends. They are low, at least, by comparison with the benefits that might be achieved from optimal use of management information in the administration of higher education. The consensus among expert observers is reflected in the recent findings of J. Victor Baldridge and Michael Tierney (1979), who evaluated the use of management-information systems in 34 private liberal-arts institutions that participated in an Exxon Education Foundation program to improve their resource allocation and management procedures. "Overall," they write, "it is our impression that management information systems... are worth their cost" (p. 13). But their study documents extensive counterproductive practices and conditions that diminish the utility of information resources as they have typically been used on campus. The tone of most of the evaluative literature is warily optimistic; good can come of it all, but only if a number of pit-falls can be avoided.

This book undertakes to describe, for the benefit of college and university administrators, who are the principal users of management information, what the author regards as the widest and deepest of those pitfalls. It is a book about basic concepts involved in the transformation of raw numbers into coherent and useful information, or knowledge. The concepts are not hard to grasp, and they are described here in plain terms. The technical task of transformation can be exceedingly complex, but the details should not concern the administrator. Only by understanding the concepts involved, however, can the administrator determine whether those who produce information intended to support important decisions are properly doing their job. More than one administrator has thumbed through a two-inch stack of incomprehensible computer printout and sadly echoed T. S. Eliot—"Where is the knowledge we have lost in information?"

Why all the difficulty in applying information technology to the administration of higher education? Raymond F. Bacchetti (1977), Vice Provost for Budget and Planning at Stanford

INTRODUCTION

University and a close student of management information and rational decision processes, makes this observation: "The first thing to be said about how decisions are made in colleges and universities is that very little is known systematically about that subject. Still less is known about how decisions ought to be made" (p. 4). That appears to be more a criticism of the state of knowledge about the art and science of administration than a criticism of information specialists. Bacchetti has a more important, if implicit, point, at least for present purposes. It is that those who design information systems and perform the analyses of data intended to generate management information frequently do not adequately or even at all understand the perspective and the information needs of the decisionmakers. Specifically, with respect to Bacchetti's observation, they do not understand how the decision at hand will be made—and, as we shall see, information needs vary, depending upon the decision process being used. Carl R. Adams (1977b), editor of a recent survey of the information needs of decisionmakers in higher education, put it this way:

Most systems development to date has been based on normative [decision] models conceptualized by researchers or technicians. While we can and should call for more research effort aimed at documenting higher education decision processes, our only short-run option for improving information systems is to encourage those with experience in administration to reflect upon and relate their views to us. [p. x]

Adams provides (1977a, pp. 81-83) a cogent compendium of expert opinion on the main sources of difficulty in meeting the information needs of administrators in higher education, as follows:

- "A reluctance on the part of management systems analysts to remain neutral in providing supporting information by defining options for the decisionmaker . . . [but instead adopting] an advocacy position for a particular decision alternative."

- "Incompatible structures for collecting information to support decisions. One is the structure used for control within the organization and the other is a structure used to analyze the outputs or accomplishments of the organization."
- "The inadequacy of the basic input/output analysis model in the light of our inability to adequately measure the outcomes of higher education. As the assessment of outcomes becomes more and more subjective, the level of accuracy appropriate in estimating resource inputs is diminished."
- "The reliance of analytical systems on the files developed for operational systems."
- "The failure of most analytical systems to synchronize the timing of the delivery of outputs to the requirements of the decision processes."
- "The relatively low level of expertise the top administrators have regarding the analytical techniques used in higher education.... The interpretors specify the information system characteristics, but they lack the perspective of the decision-maker that is necessary to focus the information requirements."

It would seem then that the quality and impact of management information in higher education will approach the ideal in proportion as we gain a better understanding of decision processes, improve the timeliness of information delivery, promote communication between administrators and data interpretors, and so on. Regrettably, that is not likely to be the case: such advances will prove more palliative than remedial, so long as the root ailment is allowed to persist. The essential difficulty is that neither administrators nor information specialists have a clear understanding of the best way to describe, in dynamic terms, the higher-education enterprise and its constituent parts. Describing decision processes in higher education much better than they are now described in the literature would help. But practicing administrators usually have a keen understanding of the processes utilized in their own institutions. Getting the information on the administrator's desk *before* the decision must be made obviously is essential. Timeliness is achieved not merely through alacrity, however, but instead through foresight—you cannot produce information from data you do not have, and you rarely can acquire new data overnight. Improved communication will help, but the administrator and the data analyst cannot exchange ideas effectively unless they share a conception of purpose and an understanding of available capabilities and limits on resources: their relationship should be closely analogous to that of the architect and the construction contractor.

The lack of a coherent conceptual foundation to guide the development of systems for collecting and storing data and for converting them into useful information in decision contexts manifests itself in many ways. It is revealed in a widespread inability to distinguish information from data and grasp the full implications of that distinction. It is implicit in a frequent failure to recognize the fundamental difference between operating data and management data. The absence of a conceptual base is a primary reason why the findings of research on decision processes have not been adequately melded with existing knowledge about the role and uses of information in decisionmaking.

We lack the needed conceptual foundation not because the component parts are unavailable, but rather because available knowledge has not been properly integrated. This book proposes a way of achieving that integration. In doing so, it discusses data and information both in definitional terms (with emphasis on their essential differences) and in functional terms. It looks at the difference between data bases that provide operational information and the kind of data base needed to produce the right kinds of management information to support administrative decisionmaking, at the right time. It surveys the uses of information and the different decision processes in which it is used. It proposes a broad framework of data needed to produce the right information at the right time, taking into account the relative unpredictability of both factors. Finally, the book looks at the human element, with emphasis on the need to develop a large cadre of information professionals—people who can *understand* the questions that administrators must answer when they make decisions and who know how to produce relevant information.

If the book realizes the author's hopes, it will leave the reader with a lively awareness that no information is better than the question that evoked it. The information professional deserves an equally adept clientele of administrators who understand what kinds of information are relevant to the decisions before them and who recognize that no accumulation of data, however comprehensive and susceptible of manipulation, can produce a *decision*. Good information can *help* the decisionmaker decide. But it must be prompted by good questions. To frame these, the administrator must have some basic knowledge about the capabilities and limitations of systems that convert data into information for the decisionmaker. Moreover, the administrator must know how to communicate with the system's proprietors. This small book is intended to impart that basic knowledge, or to refresh the understanding of those whose knowledge is rusty.

Definitions

Three terms used recurrently in the text should be at least generally defined at the outset. It already has been emphasized that a clear understanding of the difference between *data* and *information* is an absolute requirement. The distinction is so basic that system designers often neglect to state it in discussions with technically unversed system users. The third term, *strategic decisions*, does *not* refer in any specific way to *strategic planning*. Strategic planning is a management concept that takes many forms in the corporate world and is beginning to find its way into higher education, where it has provoked varying degrees of skepticism. *Strategic decision* is not a conventional term; it is used for lack of an equivalent term already established in use.

The definitions:

- *Data* are either quantities (the number of students enrolled, for example, or the number of volumes in the library) or codes—that is, numbers that identify entity characteristics, such as the race, sex, or program level of students. Data result from observation or measurement. Data are raw facts from which information can be constructed. The quality of data is determined by their validity, accuracy, and reliability, all of which are properties related to measurement.

- *Information* consists of data that have been combined and given a form in which they convey to the recipient user some useful knowledge. Information is created when data are selected, organized, and analytically manipulated, and the result is given a form that informs and serves the needs of users. The quality of information is determined by its relevance to the concerns of intended users, its timeliness, and its acceptability to users—all being properties that relate to users and the nature and context of use of information.

- *Strategic Decisions* are those concerned with questions of institutional policy, purpose, or direction. They are at a level above operational or control decisions, made routinely in the course of running the institution. They concern programs rather than courses; tenure policy rather than whether a particular faculty member should be given tenure; long-range planning rather than deciding how to implement an innovation that has been approved and budgeted. Strategic decisions most often involve executive judgments, rather than the snap judgments made in dealing with the day-to-day flow of administrative tasks. They require information produced by a *decision-support system* (see p. 35), which incorporates a *management data base* (see

p. 35). (These latter terms are defined at appropriate places in the text.)

In the next chapter, *data* is given a more thoroughgoing explication and its properties are described.

CHAPTER 2

Data

College and university administrators who wish to be well served by management information cannot be satisfied merely to know that data are fundamentally different from information. This chapter undertakes, therefore, to describe data with some precision and also describe their basic properties. It also discusses data limitations and some issues that arise when data are employed. The discussion is conceptual rather than technical, but specific nonetheless, because a root understanding of the nature of data and limitations on their use as raw material for the construction of information is needed to follow the central argument of this book. In this discussion, the author has freely applied to the context of higher-education management a number of ideas articulated by a Canadian authority on social statistics, Ivan P. Fellegi (1980)—so freely that it would clutter the text unduly to acknowledge every instance of appropriation.

Components of Data

We have noted that *data* derive from observation or measurement and take the form either of quantities (such as the number of students enrolled) or codes that identify characteristics of the entity observed or measured. (Quite arbitrarily, *data* is conventionally treated as a plural term in the literature on management information; the singular form in common use is *data item*, though *datum* occasionally appears.) An individual data item comprises more, however, than a quantity or code. It appears as a number or symbol in a specified context of meaning. That is, a data item is a measurement or observation about a particular *reference entity*, and it measures or otherwise specifies some characteristic or dimension of the reference entity. That is, it is in some clearly understood way a *descriptor*. Thus we may say that any data item, or datum, must have three basic components:

1. A *reference entity*—the thing being observed. In a student data file, the individual student is the reference entity; in a room inventory file, the room; in a library catalog, the individual volume.

2. A *descriptor* that characterizes some aspect of the reference entity. Sex, race, age, and county and state of birth are all descriptors associated with the reference entity *student*. For the reference entity *room*, area in square feet and number of seats or stations are pertinent descriptors. *Subject* is a descriptor appropriate to a library volume. *Location* and *control* are descriptors commonly associated with the reference entity *institution of higher education*.

3. A *quantity or code* that conveys the result of an observation or measurement relative to the descriptor. The codes M and F commonly record a student's sex; a number representing square feet records the area of a room; a Library of Congress call number (which in fact includes letters of the alphabet as well as digits) may record an observation about the subject matter of a book.

In short, a number or a code letter (or other symbol, such as an asterisk) is a data item only when it carries two labels—reference entity and descriptor. These labels normally are clearly specified in the titles and column headings of information reports—for example, "Undergraduate Arts and Sciences Enrollment in 1978 [entity] by Major and Class Level [descriptors]." Once recited, this notion of a data item as possessing three components of meaning, two categorical and the third either quantitative or categorical, seems only too obvious. But the fact that an individual data item can have neither more nor less than that tripartite import has great bearing on any consideration of data and its properties. Indeed, it has much to do with the character and significance of the information drawn from data, as will become clear in time.

Meanwhile, some elaboration on our definition of *reference entity* is required. So far, all of the examples offered have been single entities—one student, one room, one book. But any precisely defined group can be a reference entity. Much management information of use in higher education has to do with the behavior of groups rather than single entities—with students in various programs (history, mathematics, engineering) and at various levels (undergraduate, master's, doctoral); with instructional staff by type (tenured, nontenured, honorarium), program, and rank; with programs rather than constituent courses. If the management concern is the student pool upon which the institution draws, it may be important to have data about the income and education levels and race or ethnic characteristics of all persons residing in a particular county, state, or region. The only requirement, when the reference entity is a group, is that the group be unambiguously identified. It may be enough to clearly specify the attributes that all members of the group must share—such as residence in a particular area, attainment of a high-school diploma, or both. In another instance, it may be necessary to list the members of the group by name, as for a group consisting of all high-school graduates in 1981 who won state merit scholarships.

Again, a seemingly simple point has been spelled out. Many difficulties attributed to inaccuracies in data—improper measurement or erroneous coding—arise in fact from incomplete or variable specification of attributes that identify members of the reference entity—of the "student body," for example, or worse yet, "the faculty." Suppose a student is defined only as an individual who has registered and paid tuition and fees and faculty are defined as individuals teaching at least one course. The resulting data might be pristinely accurate, yet yield wildly misleading information about the student-faculty ratio, a commonly accepted indicator of instructional quality, or about credit-hour production per faculty member. To provide meaningful ratios of that sort, of course, data on *full-time-equivalent* students and faculty, defined in terms of course load and teaching load, must be collected. Beyond inadequate specification of reference-entity attributes, semantic and conceptual problems sometimes provoke serious misunderstandings. Suppose that classroom space is assigned with a computer program, and a class of 12 in advanced German literature is matched with a 150-seat amphitheater in the natural-sciences building. The problem is that the computer was not given adequate instructions for matching class size to space.

Implicit in the array of examples given above is this fundamental proposition:

The mere aggregation of data such that the reference entity is a group rather than an individual does not, in and of itself, yield information: rather, aggregation usually results in data about a different reference entity. Data do not become information until they have been assigned a specific context of use and (usually) analyzed appropriate to that context.

That proposition is explored at some length in the next chapter.

Properties of Data

Data have now been defined both in componential terms and with respect to their difference from information, irrespective of level of aggregation. And as we noted in the introduction, the *quality* of data has three determinants—validity, accuracy, and reliability—all of which are properties related to measurement. These terms are familiar to anyone even slightly conversant with statistics. But their implication for management information is not fully conveyed in the typical textbook definitions. When data reveal uncomfortable facts, the ensuing partisan discourse frequently is peppered with challenges to the validity, accuracy, and reliability of the data. The administrator should understand these concepts well enough to know whether or not they are being used as red herrings.

Validity concerns the extent to which the data actually measure or code what they are intended to describe. Is grade-point average a valid descriptive measure of the descriptor *academic ability*? Will a measure such as teaching load or contact hours be a valid descriptor of *faculty effort*? Does the student-faculty ratio contribute meaningfully to an assessment of *program quality*? That is, do the data we collect measure what we think we are measuring? As it happens, many essential concerns in higher education, such as program quality, have so far eluded valid measurement. At the same time, it is worth noting that in practice, validity is bestowed primarily through consensus or tacit general acceptance, particularly with respect to abstract and value-laden concepts.

A brief digression is ventured here, because program quality has become an issue of paramount concern in higher education and is likely to command attention for a long time to come. It seems safe to say that there never will be an absolute measure of the concept of program quality, just as there will never be an absolute determination of the ultimate constituents of matter. Practically speaking, however, we simply have not achieved wide acceptance for proxy measures of program quality. The great majority of faculty and administrators regard program quality as not objectively measurable. Ironically, they also are united in their conviction that program quality will suffer if it is subordinated to program efficiency, as measured by the cost of producing a student credit hour. So it seems that they are convinced they know *something* objective about program quality, if only that it has a price. Moreover, one can argue that the inability to distinguish accurately between research costs and instructional

Dennis P. Jones

costs, between educational outcomes and public service, and the interplay of countless variables in the whole process of higher education, render unit-cost calculations all but meaningless. Nonetheless, many legislators and taxpayers regard the cost of producing student credit hours as sound information. Informally in higher education, student-faculty ratios are widely accepted as rough indicators of program quality, particularly when combined with admission standards. While such indicators of educational effectiveness are no more subjective, no more political, than the practice of measuring efficiency in dollar terms, the higher-education community has been diffident about promoting consensus regarding the validity of student-faculty ratios. Presumably this state of affairs will persist until empirical evidence (obtained, perhaps, by examining the correlations of alternative measures of program quality) or legal specification (achieved, for example, when program quality is defined and its descriptors specified in a piece of federal legislation) confers validity on a particular measure or set of measures.

To sum up (somewhat truistically), be as precise as possible about what the data are to measure, and use measures whose validity has been proved empirically or is established by consensus—that is, use measures that have face validity.

Accuracy concerns precision of measurement—the disparity between an actual measurement or act of coding and a hypothetical error-free measurement or coding. There are three main sources of inaccuracy in data:

1. Error in measurement (a room was assigned an area of 620 square feet when in fact its area was 650 square feet)
2. Erroneous identification of the reference entity, either because the entity is poorly defined or was wrongly interpreted (for example, incorrectly including students enrolled only for noncredit courses in a student-body count, because either the definition of student failed to exclude people taking only noncredit courses or because the exclusion was stated but not noted by the data collector)

3. Unrepresentative sampling—a mistake in statistical analysis, rather than measurement or observation, constituting a special case of incorrect representation of the reference identity

Reliability concerns the extent to which the coding or measurement yields the same result upon repetition. A test of student achievement is considered reliable if the student receives the same score (within statistically allowable limits) on repeated applications without intervening instruction. To be reliable, coding or measurement procedures should yield identical data when performed by different individuals.

Issues Surrounding Data

The proliferation of data in our society has made inevitable the interjection of data and, on a somewhat smaller but still impressive scale, information into all manner of partisan and adversary contexts. And since data and information seldom support all positions equally, those slighted by the facts often respond in the fashion of the country lawyer who counseled: "When the evidence is against you, talk about the law. When the law is against you, talk about the evidence. When both are against you, pound on the table and shout like Hell." In our information society, as it has been dubbed, this rhetorical strategy translates roughly as follows: "If the quantitative data are against you, argue that qualitative data should have been collected. If the objective data are against you, talk about the need for subjective data. If every manner, shape, and form of data are against you, declare with feeling that values must triumph." In any case, the administrator who wishes to promote precision in communication on partisan subjects should be aware of the essential emptiness of the three issues about data most often encountered in contentious situations.

Dennis P. Jones

Misleading Data

Data that have uncomfortable implications for certain positions or raise questions about the adequacy of performance understandably may provoke the charge that "the data are misleading." But not all such charges are self-serving, and these complaints usually can be traced to concern either about validity or accuracy (as we have defined those terms). Fellegi (1980, p. 171) offers the cogent example of unemployment statistics, whose implications are variously interpreted because *unemployment* means different things to different data users. (In the United States, federal unemployment statistics refer only to people who as a matter of record are actively seeking employment. But the credibility of these statistics has diminished with the widespread realization that large numbers of long-term unemployed have given up and no longer register with employment agencies or actively seek work.) "Similarly," Fellegi writes, "unless an explicit statement about accuracy is provided, the receiver is free to assume any level for it, including 'complete accuracy.' The result may clearly be potentially misleading"—because either the descriptor ("unemployed") or the level of accuracy, or both, have been incorrectly or inadequately described.

Quantitative vs. Qualitative Data

Data are by definition inherently quantitative. A data item is a number that represents a measurement of some descriptive sort or that constitutes a code representing a categorical distinction presumably drawn on some objective ground (male or female, white, black, or Hispanic, high-school graduate or not). Therefore any characterization of data as "qualitative" amounts to one of two assertions:

1. I think data on different descriptors would be more appropriate or preferable.
2. The measure used to produce the data is not a valid descriptor—from my perspective.

With respect to the first instance, the use of unit-cost data (with a student credit hour as the unit of production) as a way of comparing two institutions often sets off cries for qualitative data about the relative effectiveness (quality) of programs at the two institutions. But the inescapable fact is that data about program quality will be quantitative and will take the form of numerical expressions of measurements. All data are fundamentally alike in that they make a concrete specification (quantity or code) with reference to a *descriptor* of a *reference entity*.

Therefore, the quantitative-qualitative distinction cannot apply to data: at best, it may be used to differentiate descriptors. It is appropriate, for example, to say that student satisfaction (expressed on a scale of one to ten) with counseling services is a qualitative descriptor and student utilization of these services (measured by average number of counseling sessions per student per year) is a quantitative descriptor. But the latter is not thereby inherently more valid; indeed, satisfaction with the process may well be a benefit in itself with respect to some forms of counseling, while student persistence in the process does not necessarily indicate either satisfaction or benefit. (One is reminded of the workman in a small town who regularly lost his wages in a Saturday night poker game in the local saloon. "Don't you know the game is crooked?" he was asked. "Sure," he replied—"but it's the only game in town.") In short, "qualitative data" and "quantitative data" are obfuscatory misnomers.

Objective vs. Subjective Data

The point at issue here involves the ways in which observations were made and the numerical values for the measures or codes obtained. Objective data derive from objective criteria; the measure was obtained free of personal feeling or perceptual idiosyncrasy, perhaps by using a weighing scale, or a tape measure. Subjective data are obtained by relying on the interpretation or judgment of the observer; a professor's grade on an essay constitutes subjective data, as do responses to yes-or-no questions about personal preferences or responses on a numerical scale to questions about political attitudes. All data eventually are reduced to quantities or codes; whether the data are subjective or objective depends on the way in which the values for the quantities or codes are generated. As one would expect, objective data generally are more reliable and more valid than subjective data. This is clearly shown in figure 1, which indicates the levels of reliability and validity associated with data of different types, data collected in different scientific disciplines, and data collected in various ways.

Validity and Reliability Ratings (Mean Rankings) for Various Types of Data, for Data in Various Scientific Disciplines, and for Data Gathered by Various Techniques

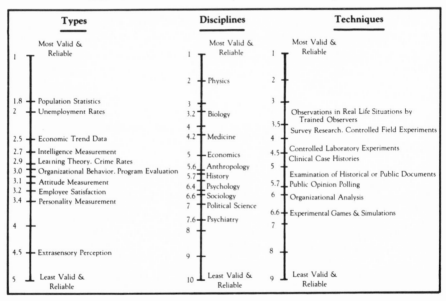

Fig. 1. [Source: Ivan P. Fellegi, "Data, Statistics, Information—Some Issues of the Canadian Social Statistics Scene" (*Statistical Reporter*, April 1980, pp. 179-81).]

DATA

Facts vs. Values

Two specialists in quantitative approaches to the management of higher education have observed that the administrator "must continually synthesize a plan of action from two aspects of reality: (1) a world of people, human values, preferences, aspirations, and interpersonal dynamics, and (2) a world of things, facts, dollars, resources, and constraints" (Lawrence and Service 1977, p. 11). Many decisionmakers tend to regard data as appropriate to the domain of things, not the domain of values. Their underlying assumption is that numbers do not convey values. The assumption is quite wrong. It is perfectly possible to acquire data about preferences, values, and aspirations, as well as about things, dollars, and resources. To be sure, value-oriented data usually derive from subjective measurement or coding, whereas data about extant dollars and resources (but not *projected* dollars and resources) are nearly always based on objective measures. But if subjective data are typically less valid and less reliable than objective data, they nonetheless can be highly informative. An ironic example is familiar to all: public-opinion polling, which mainly produces subjective data, consistently predicts how voters will divide, nationally, or state by state, or in congressional districts or other political subdivisions, within a range of plus or minus three percent. Very occasionally, nonetheless, the major polling organizations predict election results that either are flatly wrong (Truman vs. Dewey in 1948) or seem to underestimate victory margins (the Reagan "landslide" in 1980). Soulsearching by the pollsters nearly always reveals that the error was not in the data themselves, but in interpretation. The voter trend toward Truman in the final weeks of the 1948 presidential campaign was clearly shown in the data: the experts, apparently mesmerized by a media barrage on behalf of the Republican candidate, predicted a Dewey victory in the face of their own facts. In the 1980 election, the possibility that reports of Reagan victories in the eastern states (achieved within the plus-or-minus three-percent margin of polling) influenced the vote in states where the polls were still open has raised cogent questions about the causes of the unexpected sweep. But again, the polling data, although subjective, supported accurate forecasts of the actual voting in those areas where the vote could not have been influenced by television and radio election reporting.

Values can be expressed in data in at least three ways:

1. The value itself is being measured—as in data about the importance that the public assigns to environmental control.
2. Value-based observer bias influences subjective measurements.
3. Data portray facts—what *is*. Opinion about what should be—that is, how the facts should be altered at some point in the future as a result of policy decisions or actions—is shaped by the data-user's values. Distinctions between facts and values can blur, because it is both possible and often appropriate to collect data about preferences, which in effect is collecting facts about values.

In the final analysis, the ability to distinguish between facts and values should not lead to attempts to limit consideration of data to the domain of reference entities that have concrete dimension. It is fundamentally incorrect to exclude or to neglect to collect appropriate subjective data about values and perceptions. While relatively less valid and reliable than objective data, subjective data do usefully portray the state of that "world of people, human values, preferences, aspirations, and interpersonal dynamics" that the organizational decisionmaker ignores at his own peril.

The collection, storage, and retrieval of data are technical procedures, properly out of the hands of the administrators who are furnished management information. A general understanding of data—in terms of components, properties, and limitations—that this chapter has sought to impart is a necessary precursor to an understanding of the nature and uses of information, to which we now turn.

CHAPTER 3

Information

The previous chapter made mention from time to time of the uses of data. Generally in higher education, data are used by analysts to construct information for the use of administrators and other decisionmakers. Information is more difficult to define precisely than data, and it inhabits a larger, more complex, and more ambiguous domain. But the typical administrator is much better acquainted with that domain than with the domain of data. This chapter deals in somewhat more general terms, therefore, with the definitional problem, the properties of information, the kinds of information utilized by administrators, and the role that information plays in various decision processes.

Nature of Information

The author has been unable to find, in Fellegi or elsewhere in the professional literature, a definition of information nearly as precise as that provided by Fellegi for data. Lexicons are of little more help. The best of them, *Webster's Third International Dictionary,* defines information as "the communication or reception of knowledge or intelligence...knowledge obtained from investigation, study, or instruction...facts, data"—and so on. But such blurring of distinctions in a discussion of management information would undermine the whole purpose of this book. The dictionary does assign a select meaning to *information* that is more consonant with the requirements of the present discussion: "something (as a message, experimental data, or picture) which justifies change in a construct (as a plan or theory) that represents physical or mental experience or another construct." That, too, is more suggestive than concrete, however. And so, again, we will rely on Fellegi:

> Information . . . is defined as the process of conveying an interpretable message as a result of which the receiver of the message acquires knowledge, that is, becomes better informed. [1980, p. 169]

Uses of Information

The number of specific ways in which administrators might use information to advantage is well nigh limitless. Virtually all uses would find their place, however, in one or more of three categories of use: (1) decisionmaking, (2) enhancing general knowledge, (3) routing to others. If information is quickly absorbed or scanned and filed for future attention, the chances are good that in time it will impact a decision—perhaps one not envisioned when the information first came to hand. Similarly, information not absorbed beyond determining to whom it should be communicated may well in time cycle back, either by influencing the third party's position vis-a-vis some future decision or by stimulating feedback from the third party that constitutes new information. The possible permutations of use in these two categories could be ramified endlessly, but no administrator is in need of such a catalog. Students are said not to know what it is they need to know; administrators, by contrast, are acutely aware of the deficiencies in their knowledge and have a keen understanding of the benefits gained from appropriate communication of knowledge to others. Regrettably, it would be weaseling to describe some practices as "appropriate communication." Every administrator recognizes that information can constitute organizational power, particularly when access to it can be controlled in line with calculated purposes. Fortunately, the trend is away from inner-circle domination in higher-education administration and toward the open style of shared governance, which logically calls for wide dissemination of information. However, opportunities remain for artful operators to buck the trend. One such, a dean in a small college, described his tactic to Baldridge and Tierney (1979) in these words:

> People used to criticize me for not giving them enough information. Faculty members used to bombard me with complaints that I was hiding facts from them. Now I give them *all* the information—bundles and bundles and bundles. I'm hiding the real information better than I ever did before! There is so much junk that I throw at them, they can't tell the important stuff from the trivial stuff. [p. 40]

A given piece of information is important to some and trivial to others. The conscientious administrator needs no urging to route information selectively, according to the needs of recipients. Those inclined to capitalize on the power potential of information are likely to discover that in the long run, what others don't know now, they will find out eventually, sometimes to the concealer's considerable embarrassment. Data become information, then, when they are given an interpretable form and reach someone to whom their message constitutes immediately or potentially useful knowledge.

Properties of Information

The general properties of information are relevance, acceptability, timeliness, completeness, and accuracy—a set that overlaps to a considerable extent with the general properties of data—validity, accuracy, and reliability. But the properties of information are different from those of data in a cardinal respect: they are necessarily assessed relative to a group of users or a form of use; they cannot be stated in absolute terms. The properties of data are associated with measurement; the properties of information are associated with use, users, and context of use.

Relevance

The extent to which the use of a particular item of information would reduce the uncertainty associated with a specific decision determines its degree of relevance. Information projecting the undergraduate demand for physics courses in the coming semester would be highly relevant to determining teaching assignments in the physics department, somewhat relevant to a decision about whether to fill a tenure-track vacancy on the physics faculty, but of virtually no relevance in deciding whether to seek an NSF grant to finance the conversion of a nearby abandoned salt mine into a nutrino detector. In other words, relevance is a function of use, rather than an inherent property of the information itself. Why, then, refer to relevance as a property of information? We may say it is because without some degree of relevance, there can be no information—only data. With respect to its properties as well as its intrinsic nature, *information* seems always to elude exact definition.

Acceptability

The acceptability (appropriateness, communicability) of information is demonstrated by user behavior. If the receiver recognizes it as currently useful or stores it for future reference, the information has at least a nominal acceptability. If it is discarded and screened out of memory, effectively it is not information, at least not to that user. The user's acceptance or rejection should be guided by the content of the information, or determination about its relevance. But in entirely too many cases, relevant information is screened out because it does not assume a communicable form. The point needs no elaboration among administrators:

- Communication of information from analyst to user requires that they share a common language. To understand the significance of marginal-cost information to decisions about class size, an administrator must grasp the concept of marginal cost.
- Form of information is important as well as its substance. Some users prefer tables of numbers; others comprehend information only if it is presented in written form, or displayed in graphs and charts.

Again, acceptability is not an absolute property of information; what is communicable to one individual or group may miss the mark completely with another.

Timeliness

Relevant, communicable information that arrives after the decision has been made obviously can have no impact. On the other hand, timeliness of information is relative to the needs of the user and context of use. For institutional management purposes, information about expenditure levels usually cannot be more than a month old and still be maximally useful. In a research context, however, the same information can be a year old and be considered current for all intents and purposes.

Completeness

"When *all* [emphasis supplied] relevant information is included, that information is 'complete'" (Hussain 1973, p. 92). Completeness is determined relative to the theoretical set of information that would be required to reduce uncertainty in any decision situation to zero. As a practical matter, information is sufficiently complete when the administrator is satisfied that "I know all I need to know to make this decision."

Accuracy

A discussion of accuracy that embraced questions of information loss or distortion during the communication process would unavoidably become a voluminous digression. The only practical recourse is to stay as close as possible to the concept of data accuracy described in the previous chapter. Within that limitation, the criteria for accurate information may be specified as follows:

- The information must derive from accurate data
- It must have been analyzed or otherwise manipulated in such a way that the accuracy of the data is preserved
- The information must not be distorted in the communication process
- It must be interpreted by the receiver in the way intended by the provider

The Role of Information in Decisionmaking

The professional literature seeking to describe, analyze, and assess the decision processes in business and government is portly; the literature on decisionmaking in higher education is thin, but rapidly putting on weight. One may argue that the paucity results from the relatively slow pace of development of management-information systems in colleges and universities, or conversely that the development has been slowed by the lack of knowledge about how to apply decision information in higher education—knowledge that ought to have been generated by more R&D. Both propositions no doubt are at least partly correct. However that may be, the general tendency, when data-processing technology began to take hold on campus, was to regard management information (which, as we have noted, often was merely recycled operational data) as primarily relevant to and conducive of so-called rational decisionmaking. The trouble was, and is, that no one has been able to isolate an instance of provably unadulterated rational decisionmaking, either in higher education or in any other sector of our society. We have been content to say here that the decisionmaker undoubtedly would welcome that complete set of purely relevant information that would reduce to zero the uncertainty involved in making a significant decision—but knows that no such set of information can be acquired. Various theorists argue, moreover, that information is susceptible of misuse, deliberate and otherwise, in all manner of ways. It may be misinterpreted, partially or wholly concealed, inadequately communicated among decision participants, and so on. And we have noted that the role of information in decisionmaking may be challenged by interests it appears to misserve.

Nonetheless, information increasingly is being applied in various decision processes in higher education, and the influence of process on use deserves some mention here. The literature offers a number of descriptive models of how decisions get made. The formal model, so called, views decisionmaking as a rational, problem-solving process: a problem is identified, information is collected, alternatives are formulated and evaluated, and the best alternative is selected based on an assessment of the likely consequences of that choice (MacCrimmon and Taylor 1977). Baldridge (1971) argues that decision processes are full of conflict, and primarily *political* in nature. He holds that interest groups put such pressure on decisionmakers that they tend to use information only to the extent that it buttresses their position. Choices are political compromises, Baldridge maintains, and thus decisionmaking is essentially a political art. Millett (1962) describes and argues for *collegial* decision processes in which participants have equal voice, share expertise, and achieve resolution through collective (and consensual) judgments. Weber

Dennis P. Jones

(1947) described *bureaucratic* processes by which decisions are achieved through the application of carefully prescribed policies, procedures, and decision criteria. Cohen, March, and Olsen (1972) offer the analogy of a "garbage can" from which decisions gradually emerge, not as a result of formal calculation but through a complicated process of mixing problems, solutions, participants, and choice opportunities. Finally, decision processes may be simply *autocratic*—the work of a single decision-maker. (In higher education, the autocratic process is rarely used to reach nontrivial decisions.) The critical point is all of these processes are regularly found in most organizations and that the kind of information used is different for each process. Only when a decision becomes programmed—that is, when it is reached through a bureaucratic process—can information requirements be specified with little uncertainty.

Present purposes do not require further consideration of these alternative models of the decision process. It is enough to observe that the kind of information employed in resolving any particular problem depends heavily on the decision process used. Let us take as an example the problem of establishing tuition levels for the coming year. In a private institution, presumably those involved in the decision would seek information about such things as the projected need for tuition revenues, the relationship between tuition levels and tuition income in past years, the economic circumstances of enrolled students and their ability to pay, tuition levels at competing institutions, and the student-aid picture. Tuition being a relatively more important source of revenue in the private sector than in the public sector, one would expect to find a concomitant tendency toward rational, information-oriented decisions about tuition levels, albeit with some variation in the extent of information use, depending on the decision process employed. In a state where tuition levels for public institutions are tied by formula to a calculated cost of education, information needs will be entirely different. The formula constitutes a bureaucratic decision process: the only information required is that reflecting institutional costs. In some states, tuition levels are established by an annual act of the legislature. This involves an intensely complicated decision process with innumerable participants and a spectrum of information that might range from the cost of living in the state to comparative figures on tuition levels in neighboring states to statistics on out-migration of the state's high-school graduates.

The next chapter considers some general characteristics of information needs in higher education, and then we look at the multiplicity of types of information that administrators need and how one goes about specifying the content of a comprehensive management data base. For now, we will sum up our discussion of information with a matrix (figure 2) in which are shown the different kinds of information used in the four primary decision-making models described previously (the seldom-used autocratic model is omitted) and the different uses to which the information is put. The matrix is mainly the work of Ellen Chaffee of the National Center for Higher Education Management Systems, who has closely studied decision processes in higher education.

Role of Information in Decisionmaking

Information Considerations	Decisionmaking Models			
	Formal	Collegial	Bureaucratic	Political
• Who collects, prepares, presents information?	Professional analysts, substantive experts	Everyone	Administrators throughout the organization (mainly at lower & mid levels) assigned this role	Anyone with a position to advocate or refute
• Who uses information in the course of decisionmaking?	Line authorities	Everyone, collegium	Specific administrators	Partisans
• What determines kind of information needed?	Problem definition	Problem definition	Procedure, precedent	Partisan debate and negotiation
• What is "information," in the context of the model?	Verifiable facts, probabilistic analyses, expert judgment	Verifiable facts, probabilistic analyses, expert judgment, persuasive rhetoric	Verifiable facts (digested & presented according to routines)	Verifiable facts, probabilistic analyses, persuasive rhetoric
• When is information used?	Early in stages of problem-solving; continuously only through choice	Early in stages of problem-solving; continuously only through choice	Regularly, as determined by standard operating procedures	Early in the process of issue identification; continuously only through choice
• What issues does information address?	Costs and benefits of choice alternatives	Relative validity of alternatives as means to agreed-on objectives	Issues historically and continually established by the organization	Mutual benefits of an alternative
• How is information intended to support logic behind the decision model?	To identify the alternatives with maximum cost-benefits	To iterate toward consensus	To identify current state of traditional decision premises	To persuade contenders toward a self-interested favorable outcome
• How significant is the role of information in determining the decision?	Critical— no decision possible without it	Very important (but so is a colleague's opinion)	May be important (a) for direct use in making a decision and/or (b) for organizational continuity and stability, but not for decisions	Very important (although indirect) effect on decision in that it helps determine actors' positions

Fig. 2. (Developed at NCHEMS by Ellen Chaffee.)

CHAPTER 4

The Management Data Base

From the previous chapters on data, information, and their respective properties, it is essential to bring forward two points: (1) data are raw material for information, and (2) a specific information need is determined by who will use it and for what purpose. In this chapter, we will distinguish between two kinds of management information—that which supports day-to-day operation decisions and that which supports management control and strategic decisions. Then we will consider the implications of that distinction for the development of data bases and also the development of systems that transform data into different kinds of information. Considerable attention is given to the characteristics of the data necessary to support strategic decisions.

By way of preface to this chapter, we must clear away another bit of semantic underbrush: a *data base* is not the same thing as an *information system*. A data base is a repository for quantified or encoded facts, regardless of whether the facts describe entities consisting of individuals or of groups. An information system is a means for drawing raw numbers from one or more data bases and converting them into information.

Dennis P. Jones

Management Information Needs

In the previous chapter, much was made of the fact that an information need is a function of use, user, and context. Reviewed in detail, the varieties of management activity and information use seem virtually infinite. However, Anthony (1965) put forward a tripartite classification that has proved generally useful in categorizing the extensive range of possibilities:

- "Strategic planning [or, in the technology of this book, strategic decisionmaking] is the process of deciding on objectives of the organization, on changes in these objectives, on the resources used to attain these objectives, and on the policies that are to govern the acquisition, use, and disposition of these resources" (p. 24)
- Management control is "the process by which managers assure that resources are obtained and used effectively and efficiently in the accomplishment of the organization's objectives" (p. 27)
- Operational control is "the process of assuring that specific tasks are carried out effectively and efficiently" (p. 69)

Gorry and Scott Morton (1971) have observed that the "information requirements of these three activities...are very different from one another. Further, this difference is not simply a matter of aggregation, but one of fundamental character of the information needed by managers in these areas" (p. 57).

This contention is given credence by figure 3, in which are displayed the characteristics of information required for different categories of managerial activity according to Gorry and Scott Morton (1971, p. 59). (In figure 3, the arrows denote the continuum, and the characterizations of information in the strategic-planning column are not absolute but relative: planning information, for example, is "quite old" only by comparison with operational information.)

By extension, figure 3 also provides the basis for characterizing two quite different kinds of data bases and associated information systems. On the one hand are the data bases and systems that support operational decisions; these are typically referred to as operational, or transactional, systems. They utilize data that (1) are generated internally by the institution, (2) are detailed with respect to the object of their focus, and (3) are used in ways that place a premium on currency and accuracy (payrolls cannot even be a day late or a dollar off). The related information systems tend to be narrowly defined (admissions systems, payroll systems), to be used frequently, and to function in an environment of relative certainty. We know what we want operational information systems to do, and the reports they generate next month will be the same in form and use as those generated this month. These characteristics furnish incentive to invest in systems that are rigorously defined and greatly efficient regarding both storage and processing of data.

Characteristics of Information
Required for Different Managerial Activities

Characteristics of Information	Operational Control	Management Control	Strategic Planning
Source	Largely internal ——————————→		External
Scope	Well defined, narrow ——————→		Very wide
Level of Aggregation	Detailed ———————————————→		Aggregate
Time Horizon	Historical ——————————————→		Future
Currency	Highly current ———————————→		Quite old
Required Accuracy	High ————————————————————→		Low
Frequency of Use	Very frequent ———————————→		Infrequent

Fig. 3. [Source: G. Anthony Gorry and Michael S. Scott Morton, "A Framework for Management Information Systems" (*Sloan Management Review* 13 [Fall 1971]:59).]

At the other end of the spectrum are data bases and information systems that support strategic decisionmaking; these are significantly different from operational systems. The data bases contain data of much greater scope but less detail. Many of the data are generated externally to the institution—for example, by the Bureau of Labor Statistics, the Department of Commerce, or the American Association of University Professors. For these and other reasons, the data are often less accurate and less current than internally generated data. Moreover, the information systems that support strategic decisionmaking function in a context markedly different from that in which operational decisions are made.

Simon (1977, p. 46) analyzed the contextual differences in terms of *programmed* and *nonprogrammed* decisions. Operational information systems support programmed decisions for which "a definite procedure has been worked out for handling them so that they don't have to be treated *de novo* each time they occur." Strategic decisions, on the other hand, are nonprogrammed— "novel, unstructured and consequential." Simon adds: "There is no cut and dried method of handling the problem because it hasn't arisen before or because its precise nature and structure are elusive or complex or because it is so important that it deserves a custom tailored treatment." In short, the data bases and related information systems that support strategic decisions must be designed to produce information relevant to decisions that are unpredictable, as to both specific substance and timing. Even when particular kinds of decisions, such as those that shape annual budgets, must be made at stated intervals, the decision process is likely to vary from year to year, and with it the information required. When output requirements for the information system are unpredictable and nonrepetitive, the major design criteria become flexibility and ease of access, rather than speed and efficiency. A premium is placed on an information professional who can "reach into the data base and pull out the combination of data that serves the particular need."

With this background, additional terminology can now be introduced.

Operational (transactional) data base—the set of data, usually generated internally, that supports the day-in, day-out repetitive processes of the institution.

THE MANAGEMENT DATA BASE

Operational information system—the means by which transactional data are processed to yield regular reports of predetermined content, to guide day-to-day operational decisionmaking (monthly expenditure reports, course-enrollment information, payroll information).

Management data base—the set of data necessary to support strategic decisions. Some of the data incorporated in management data bases are derived from operational data bases; these are augmented, however, by many kinds of data originating outside the institution. The data in management data bases typically are more aggregate and are updated less frequently than the data in operational data bases.

Decision-support system—the mechanism by which management data are transformed into information required for strategic decisionmaking.

Management-information system (MIS) is a familiar term in most administrative circles, but it is too broad to be useful in this document. It is commonly used to denote information systems that draw on various data bases to construct predetermined kinds of information. Such systems often have little or no capacity to respond to ad hoc requests. Thus they are more like what we have called operational information systems. However, *MIS* often is used broadly to encompass what we have called decision support systems. So we will avoid ambiguity by consistent usage of more precise alternative terms and eschew MIS altogether.

The balance of this chapter is given over to an in-depth discussion of management data systems.

Criteria for Management Data Bases

The foregoing brief overview implies design criteria for management data bases. They must be broad in the scope of their data content, but deal with aggregates rather than details. The required scope usually must be achieved at the expense of currency and accuracy, because much required data will originate outside the institution. The system drawing on the management data base is expected to produce information less frequently and regularly than is the case for operational systems, and the specifics of information required may be largely unpredictable. In designing management data bases, the emphasis should be on flexibility and ease of access or retrieval, with less attention given to storage or processing efficiencies, which are important in operational (transactional) systems.

The key design issue inheres in the fact that information needs relative to strategic and control decisions frequently change so rapidly, and sometimes so drastically, that past needs are poor predictors of future needs. Particularly in the situation of financial stress and enrollment decline bedeviling so many colleges and universities today, time constraints too often do not allow the accumulation of requisite data after the problem to be addressed has been identified. More often than not, information used in any particular decision context is constructed out of whatever data lie ready to hand.

The present writer is convinced that the best way to approach the design of a management data base is to proceed deductively, taking guidance from a generalized descriptive model of a higher-education institution and its environment. This is not to argue that a single, centrally designed data base can be utilized by all institutions. It is possible, however, to put forward a general descriptive model within which selections of data appropriate to the needs of individual institutions can be made. Such an approach has several advantages in addition to its realistic recognition that information requirements fluctuate. These advantages include:

- *Breadth of Perspective*: Through use of a descriptive model (such as the one proposed below), attention is directed to external-environment matters critical to strategic decisions
- *Attention to Interrelationships*: Since data come to management data bases from many sources, systems design must focus on their use in interrelated ways

THE MANAGEMENT DATA BASE

- *Focus on the Management Data System as a Separate Entity*: Design of a management data base using a descriptive concept (rather than existing data sources) as a starting point helps ensure that the necessary difference between decision-support systems and operational systems is not inadvertently compromised

The Proposed Model

The generalized descriptive model proposed below as a guide to the development of a management data base for a particular institution suggests two basic stages of systems development. First, the major *reference entities* —individuals, groups, organizations—about which data should be included, are identified. Then the appropriate *descriptors* for each of the reference entities should be determined.

Reference Entities

For any given institution, a multitude of entities exists about which data might be considered for inclusion in a management data system. Most important, of course, is the *institution* itself. This is the entity given predominant attention in most data systems, sometimes almost to the exclusion of others. The next most important entity is the *student body*. In many data systems, student data are treated as a component of the set of data describing the institutional entity. Institutions would be better served if students were regarded for all purposes as a separate reference entity. The third large reference entity of major concern to institutions of higher education consists of the various *critical constituents*—the interest groups in the external environment that may have immediate and direct impact on, or receive impact from, the institution. This third entity, actually a group of similar entities, includes agencies of state and federal governments, philanthropic organizations and private donors, employers of graduates, and accrediting and professional associations, to name a few. Their influence is directly exercised through either funding or regulatory mechanisms. They benefit directly from the services or goods produced by the institution. Entities in the proximate environment that directly impact the institution often have similar relationships with students—a cardinal example being funders who provide both institutional grants and student aid.

The basic framework for the descriptive model thus consists of the institution, its students, and related interest groups. As figure 4 shows, each basic entity is part of a larger entity that must in some degree be described in the system if it is to accommodate, in broad outline, all the data that a comprehensive management data system should incorporate.

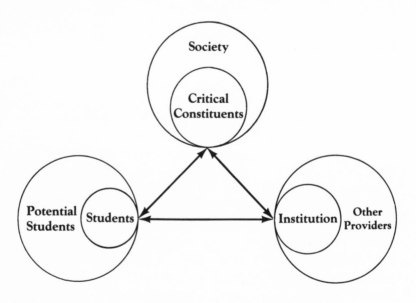

Fig. 4: Basic Entities of the System of Higher Education

THE MANAGEMENT DATA BASE

The institution is concerned with other providers of education because virtually every college and university competes with and cooperates with at least a few other organizations providing learning opportunities. The model therefore is expanded to include *other providers*, with the specification that the term includes not only traditional institutions of higher education but such other providers as proprietary institutions, the military, professional associations, business, government agencies, and religious and social organizations.

An institution's students constitute a subset of *potential students*. Within the institution's service area, the potential student body typically comprises a number of identifiable subgroups. But not every individual captured in these groups is in reality a prospective student, and for a given institution, only selected subgroups are really probable sources of students. Subgroups of the potential-student entity vary by institution and can be characterized in many ways—by age, prior education, economic status, occupation, and so on.

Society, the entity that envelopes the institution's critical constituents, admittedly is an unwieldy abstraction, but one that must be accommodated in an effective management data system. (This entity also has been termed the *remote environment*, which is not less abstract.) The impacts of society on the institution (and vice versa) are seldom so direct as those of the interest groups in the proximate environment; societal impact nonetheless remains both important and pervasive. The society entity embraces such factors as the economy (inflation, employment), public attitudes about higher education, and the general political environment for higher education. These and innumerable related factors operate as truly independent variables with respect to institutional planning and management decisionmaking: a college or university executive can do little or nothing about them. And their influence cannot be safely ignored, as the uneven course of higher education in this country since the sixties attests. The management data system that ignores societal variables is incomplete; commonly in higher education, the economy is regarded as the most important of these variables.

Descriptors of Reference Entities

The first step in the design of a management data system has not been completed until the identification of specific entities has been carried to feasible limits within the six-element model depicted in figure 4. Step two is to identify what needs to be known about each specific reference entity, specified in terms of quantitative measures and coded characteristics. The set of specific entities lodged in each of the six elements of the model will vary extensively from one institution to another. A generalized discussion of descriptors therefore may appear to hold little promise for useful concreteness: one can hardly determine how best to describe a specific entity until it has been identified. Nonetheless, some generalizations about categories of descriptors and the specific descriptors these categories include is advisable.

As with the model used to support step-one development, a framework for descriptors can guide the deductive developmental effort called for in step two. Again, we should expect from a uniformly applicable categorization scheme the conceptual virtues of simplicity and symmetry, conducing to a streamlined data-base design. All potentially valuable descriptors of all the major entities should be accommodated. The framework should consist of categories that apply uniformly to the assemblage of entities. Moreover, it should group descriptors in ways that yield useful conceptual insights while at the same time facilitating the operational aspects of data-system design and development. Three overarching categories of descriptors are proposed: identifiers, state (condition), and program.

THE MANAGEMENT DATA BASE

Identifiers

These descriptors are needed to unambiguously specify the reference entity. Where the entity is an individual or institution, identifiers include such descriptors as name and address. If the reference entity is a group, whether of individuals or organizations, common characteristics of members (black students, two-year public colleges) are used to specify it. For individuals, traits such as age, sex, educational background, and place of residence are commonly specified. For institutions, control and type of institution are typical identifiers. Such traits seldom change.

State or Condition

These descriptors establish the circumstance or status of the reference entity at some point in time: they might also be labeled *asset* descriptors. Within this category, it is helpful to identify three subcategories:

- *Internal States or Conditions*—states that inhere in the entity at a given time. For example, an individual's level of knowledge in a particular area or beliefs and attitudes are descriptors of that individual's internal state at some point in time—what the entity is.
- *External Assets*—the set of resources (financial, physical, human, informational) under the control of the entity at a point in time—this subcategory describes what the entity has.
- *Relationship States or Conditions*—the state of association between one entity and others (for example, membership status of an individual vis-a-vis a professional association, or of an institution vis-a-vis an accreditation agency).

Program

This category includes descriptors of the strategies or activities pursued by an entity in order to accomplish a desired change (or

Dennis P. Jones

maintain a desired status quo) in state or condition, for itself or for any other entity. Program descriptors tell what the entity *does*; they summarize activity over a given period of time—in colleges and universities, usually a semester, an academic year, or a fiscal year. The following subcategories are needed to describe programs:

- *Purposes*—which conditions (internal or external assets or relationships) are to be changed or maintained. Purposes are synonymous with intended outcomes.
- *Target Entity*—the entity in which the change in condition or state specified in *purposes* is intended to occur.
- *Method*—the means or mechanisms to be employed in accomplishing change in condition or state. For an institution, the method of creating internal change in students might be, for example, laboratory experience, group discussion, or work experiences. For a state agency, the method employed in carrying out a program is typically the distribution of resources or the imposition of regulatory requirements.
- *Level of Activity*—a descriptor of *how much* activity is proposed or was engaged in over the period of time in order to accomplish the intended change in the target entity. The number of student credit hours taught in a semester or year is a common indicator of level of activity in instructional programs.
- *Resources*—descriptors of the amounts of resources (human, financial, physical) allocated, expended, or utilized to carry out any particular program.
- *Outcomes*—the changes in condition or state that accrue to any entity (either intended or unintended) as a consequence of the programs.
- *Beneficiary Entity*—identifies the entity in which a change in condition or state actually did occur.

THE MANAGEMENT DATA BASE

To sum up, a management data base in higher education must accommodate three kinds of reference entities—students/potential students, institutions/other providers, critical constituents/society—and three kinds of descriptors—identifier, state, and program. We must add the dimension of time: data on the state, or condition, of a reference entity—students, for example—describes that state at a particular time. Comparison of such data with parallel data collected at a different time is one means of producing information about change in state. The underlying point is that a management data base should yield information about the dynamics of the system of interrelations that embraces the institution, its students, and the world about them.

From this point of development on, in any given institutional application, our model would rapidly lose its generality as the administrator and analyst draped lists of specific data requirements over its conceptual parts. This is one good reason for eschewing here the task of writing out those laundry lists—the lists will significantly and sometimes radically differ from one institution to another. Another reason for not attempting such a compilation is that the state of knowledge is not uniformly complete, once we venture beyond the conceptual and general. The author is among several researchers, informally affiliated through their membership in the Association for the Study of Higher Education, who at this writing are undertaking a wide-ranging compilation of data needs to provide a full spectrum of management information in higher-education settings. The hope is to develop a comprehensive and detailed scheme for describing higher education dynamically and in all its essentials—one that researchers and administrators alike will find sufficiently realistic and complete to serve as a standard. This will take a good deal of time. But so does the development of a management data base at an institution. Much of the requisite data, particularly in the student area, has long been collected by virtually all institutions and put to various informational uses. This book describes what the author believes to be a conceptual framework that will not be soon out-dated. It should prove adequate to accommodate the results of present efforts to specify what data are needed to generate all the various kinds of information that college and university administrators might require.

Previous disavowals of intent to dwell on details in this book notwithstanding, the administrator may still welcome some demonstration of how the management data base modeled here would be put to use by the data analysts. As articulated to this point, the model suggests six general subjects about which analysis might be undertaken to produce information required by an administrator. They include student-institution relationships; the state (or condition) of students, interest groups, financing, and institutional assets; and the allocation and utilization of assets. For the sake of illustration, we will consider just one of the many questions asked by decisionmakers at almost all institutions with respect to student-institution relationships: "Who are our students?"

The analyst's task appears relatively simple—first to call up from the data base the available descriptive statistics about current students. The analyst then sorts through these to select a subset of descriptors that will most usefully characterize the major groups of students currently enrolled. Typically, it is most profitable to look at such identifiers as age, sex, race, and such state descriptors as geographic origin, prior education, employment status, socioeconomic background, and academic ability (as measured by test scores, high-school ranking, or other descriptors deemed appropriate).

At this point, the analyst's task has lost its appearance of simplicity. These data can be combined in an enormous number of different ways to describe various groups within the student body along a considerable number of dimensions. "Who are our students?" turns out to be an omnibus question: "What is the ethnic composition of our student body? How do the various ethnic groups compare with respect to academic preparation?

THE MANAGEMENT DATA BASE

Socioeconomic background? Program preference?"—and so on and so on.

To confront an administrator with a pile of reports displaying these data in all their conceivably informative permutations would be in itself nearly always a useless activity, because few administrators have either the time or inclination to sift through hundreds of pages of computer printout in search of information of significance. A management data base may be an illuminating beacon, or it may be a perverse cornucopia, spewing out indigestible numbers. Clearly, the analyst should understand beforehand *why* the administrator wants to know "Who are our students?" Is the institution concerned about equal access? About matching program mix to student needs? Is there concern to know in what major respects the student body has changed over the last five years? *Since data become information only in a context of use, the data analyst must understand that context in order to produce useful information.* In the next and concluding chapter, this observation is reiterated and somewhat expanded upon.

CHAPTER 5

Concluding Observations

A Summation

The Book of Proverbs admonishes that repetition is the death of friendship. Therefore the conventional concluding summary of what has been said will be confined to three sentences: There are significant conceptual differences between data and information. The need for information is a function not only of use, but of user and context. Information needed to support strategic decisionmaking is different in significant ways from that which supports operational management.

It remains to consider three important consequences of those statements. (This consideration may be aided at the outset by a look at figure 4, which may be regarded as a data-to-information flow model, providing an organizing structure for the content of the earlier chapters on data and information.)

First, because the content and working characteristics of operational systems and decision-support systems are so different, they should be developed as separate but interdependent (rather than integrated) systems. The decision-support system is best designed as a stand-alone, complete system that incorporates what we have called a *management data base*—one that taps multiple data sources, including the institution's operational data base.

Second, there is no sound choice but to build a general-purpose decision-support system that can respond to demands for a wide variety of information, often requiring unpredictable combinations of data. Precisely because the design cannot incorporate a predetermined set of analytic procedures and matching data that will meet all information requirements, it is most fruitful to design the system around a descriptive model of the college or university and its environment. Obviously, a descriptive, conceptually based system runs the risk of being nonselective, of encompassing at least some data that will remain in the nice-to-know category rather than being demonstrably necessary. Without the exercise of considerable acute judgment, however, the tendency will be to collect and retain too much data, no matter how the design process is initiated. In the judgment of the present writer, a design that starts from a sound conceptual base is far less likely to contain extraneous elements than one that starts from other premises.

The third major consequence of the summary statements above was alluded to at the close of the last chapter: successful design of a management data base requires a competent information specialist—a professional, not merely a technician—between the data and the information. A small expansion on this point will bring us to the end of this short treatise.

The Human Element

The transformation of data into information that is both relevant and communicable to the user is never a solely mechanical task. The information professional must be sophisticated about data and its analytic treatment, certainly—but in addition must have a threefold ability: (1) to understand the management problem, (2) to appreciate the perspective from which the user addresses the problem, and (3) to identify and appropriately analyze the data that will best inform the user confronting the problem. Such capacities are not built into the data base and cannot be incorporated in analytic software. They must reside in an individual—a professional of a sort too seldom found in higher education. Regard, as Baldridge and Tierney did, the all-too-typical experience of one small institution, described by its dean:

> We worked hard to develop a first-class data base and an excellent software system. But in spite of that, in the early stages we had a hell of a problem getting the appropriate information. After a while we realized the difficulty: the project director was giving us answers to questions we weren't asking! And, more often than not, when we asked a question, he did not furnish appropriate data. He had his own idea of what we needed and was giving us tons of information about it. But we usually wanted something else.... Finally the president called the committee together and for about six weeks we thrashed through the kinds of information we needed and wanted. We insisted that the *amount* be reduced and the *focus* be on things we really needed. After that the situation got dramatically better. [1979, p. 42]

The ideal information professional has been described by Sheehan as one "sufficiently versatile to assume the perspectives of three people: (1) the decision-maker, such as the president or the academic senate, asking for information and choosing to use it for decision-making; (2) the analyst, wearing his or her own hat and translating the information needed into terms that will admit a solution—that is, taking into account the imprecision of the question, inadequacies of the data base, limitations of available tools and techniques, time, talent, and other resources for proper analysis; and (3) the technician to whom the practice and technical aspects of gathering information are clear and the meaning of the resultant data unmistakable." Sheehan adds: "The effectiveness of the communication between the analyst and the decision-maker depends on the confidence they have in each other" (1977, p. 93).

All this may be taken to indicate that the prospects for improved design and use of management data bases in higher education are severely limited by the short supply of people with the right combination of skills, intellect, insight, and experience.

It is correct to conclude that only such people can substantially improve the present deficient state of management information available on the typical American campus. Some administrators try to double as their own information specialists. They often succeed to the extent that they frame excellent questions—only to fail when they venture over to the computer center and seek the answers. The usual mistake is to make ill-informed requests for data—data that are not available, or not compatible with other data requested, or not the best source of the desired information. Such requests often cause organizational chaos and create dissatisfactions to no purpose: a knowledgeable analyst either could have obtained the right data without trouble, or would have known at the outset that in view of the data and time available, the administrator's questions could not be answered—and would have said so.

It is wrong to believe that the supply of able analysts must remain short. Competent informational professionals are made, not born, and many are self-made. If sound concepts underlie their training and practice, they will increase in number and grow in ability. Administrators who understand and champion sound concepts, and who refuse to settle for less, can create the motivation and the job opportunities that will attract competent people into the information profession. If this does not happen, information for control and strategic decisions will not improve in quality or impact. But neither will the printing out of numbers at the computer center lessen in volume.

BIBLIOGRAPHY

Adams, Carl R. "Information Technology: Performance and Promise." In *Appraising Information Needs of Decision Makers*, pp. 79-87. New Directions for Institutional Research, no. 15. Edited by Carl R. Adams. San Francisco: Jossey-Bass, 1977a.

Adams, Carl R., ed. *Appraising Information Needs of Decision Makers*. New Directions for Institutional Research, no. 15. San Francisco: Jossey-Bass, 1977b.

Anthony, Robert. *Planning and Control Systems: A Framework for Analysis*. Cambridge, Mass.: Harvard Business School, 1965.

Arns, Robert G. "Characteristics of Universities: Implications for Information Systems." University of Vermont, Burlington, Vermont, 5 November 1978.

Astin, Alexander W. "Student-Oriented Management: A Proposal for Change." In *Evaluating Educational Quality: A Conference Summary*, pp. 3-18. Washington, D.C.: Council on Postsecondary Accreditation, 1979.

Bacchetti, Raymond F. "In Praise of Good Questions." In *Appraising Information Needs of Decision Makers*, pp. 11-18. New Directions for Institutional Research, no. 15. Edited by Carl R. Adams. San Francisco: Jossey-Bass, 1977.

Baldridge, J. Victor. *Power and Conflict in the University: Research in the Sociology of Complex Organizations*. New York: Wiley, 1971.

BIBLIOGRAPHY

Baldridge, J. Victor, and Tierney, Michael L. *New Approaches to Management.* San Francisco: Jossey-Bass, 1979.

Bell, Daniel. "Welcome to the Post-Industrial Society." *Physics Today* 29 (February 1976):46-49.

Bess, James L. "Classroom and Management Decisions Using Student Data." *Journal of Higher Education* 50 (May/June 1979):256-79.

Bonner, James T.; Duncan, Joseph W.; Goldstein, Harold; and Hagan, Robert L. "Policy Relevance and the Integrity of Statistics." *Statistical Reporter*, January 1980, pp. 64-69.

Brooks, Lester. "Method to Their Madness: Harnessing Creativity." *TWA Ambassador*, November 1978, p. 112.

Casaday, Gailyn D. "Cornell's Old Girl Network and Organizational Change: 1906-1921." *Review of Higher Education* 3 (Spring 1980):19-23.

Cohen, Michael D., March, James G., and Olsen, Johan P. "A Garbage Can Model of Organizational Choice." *Administrative Science Quarterly* 17 (March 1972):1-25.

Davis, Gary. "Institutional Research and External Agency Reporting Responsibility." *The AIR Professional File* 8 (Winter 1980-81):1-4.

Dressel, Paul L., and Associates. *Institutional Research in the University: A Handbook.* San Francisco: Jossey-Bass, 1971.

Duncan, Joseph W. "Recent Developments in Reorganization of Statistical Policy." *Statistical Reporter*, April 1980, pp. 157-67.

BIBLIOGRAPHY

Fellegi, Ivan P. "Data, Statistics, Information—Some Issues of the Canadian Social Statistics Scene." *Statistical Reporter*, April 1980, pp. 168-81.

Gardner, Don E., and Parker, John D. "MIS in Higher Education: A Reassessment." *Cause/Effect* 1 (May 1978):10.

Gorry, G. Anthony, and Scott Morton, Michael S. "A Framework for Management Information Systems." *Sloan Management Review* 13 (Fall 1971):55-70.

Hefferlin, J. B. Lon, and Phillips, Ellis L., Jr. *Information Services for Academic Administration.* San Francisco: Jossey-Bass, 1971.

Heydinger, Richard B., and Norris, Donald M. "Decentralized or Centralized Systems for Colleges and Universities?" *Cause/Effect* 2 (September 1979):2-7.

Hussain, Khateeb M. *Development of Information Systems for Education.* Englewood Cliffs, N.J.: Prentice-Hall, 1973.

"Improving the Federal Statistical System: Report of the President's Reorganization Project for the Federal Statistical System." *Statistical Reporter*, May 1980, pp. 197-214.

Jonsen, Richard W. *State Policy Issues Affecting Independent Higher Education.* Research report from State-National Information Network. Washington, D.C.: Office of Research, National Institute of Independent Colleges and Universities, [1980].

Lawrence, G. Ben, and Service, Allan L., eds. *Quantitative Approaches to Higher Education Management: Potential, Limits, and Challenge.* ERIC/Higher Education Research Report, no. 4. Washington, D.C.: American Association for Higher Education, 1977.

BIBLIOGRAPHY

Lenning, Oscar T.; Lee, S.; Micek, Sidney S.; and Service, Allan L. *A Structure for the Outcomes of Postsecondary Education.* Boulder, Colo.: National Center for Higher Education Management Systems, 1977.

Litten, Larry H. "Marketing Higher Education: Benefits and Risks for the American Academic System." *Journal of Higher Education* 51 (January/February 1980):40-59.

London, Herbert I. "Loyalists vs. Shakers: The Campus Battle Is Joined." *The Chronicle of Higher Education*, 3 November 1980, p. 25.

MacCrimmon, Kenneth R., and Taylor, Ronald N. "Decision Making and Problem Solving." In *Handbook of Industrial and Organizational Psychology*, pp. 1397-1453. Edited by Marvin D. Dunnette. Chicago: Rand McNally, 1977.

McDonough, A. M. *Information Economics and Management Systems.* New York: McGraw-Hill, 1963.

Meadow, Charles T. *The Analysis of Information Systems.* 2nd ed. Los Angeles, Calif.: Melville Publishing, 1973.

Millett, John D. *The Academic Community.* New York: McGraw-Hill, 1962.

Peng, Samuel S. *HEGIS Post-Survey Validation Study: Summary Report.* Rockville, Md.: WESTAT, [1979].

Peters, Thomas J. "Putting Excellence into Management." *Business Week*, 21 July 1980, p 196-205.

Rockart, John F. "Chief Executives Define Their Own Data Needs." *Harvard Business Review*, March/April 1979, pp. 81-93.

BIBLIOGRAPHY

St. John, Edward P. "MIS Development in Higher Education: A Framework for Systems Planning." Paper presented at the 19th annual conference of the Association of Institutional Research, San Diego, California, 13-17 May 1979.
Arlington, Va.: ERIC Document Reproduction Service, ED 171 348.

Saunders, Laura E. "Dealing with Information Sytems: The Institutional Researcher's Problems and Prospects." *The AIR Professional File* 2 (Summer 1979):1-4.

Schmidtlein, F. A. "Information Systems and Concepts of Higher Education Governance." In *Appraising Information Needs of Decision Makers*, pp. 29-42. New Directions for Institutional Research, no. 15. Edited by Carl R. Adams. San Francisco: Jossey-Bass, 1977.

Schoedenbeck, P. P., ed. *Management Systems: A Book of Readings*. New York: John Wiley and Sons, 1968.

Sheehan, Bernard S. "Reflections on the Effectiveness of Informational Support for Decision Makers." In *Appraising Information Needs of Decision Makers*, pp. 89-102. New Directions for Institutional Research, no. 15. Edited by Carl R. Adams. San Francisco: Jossey-Bass, 1977.

Sheldon, Eleanor Bernert, and Parke, Robert. "Social Indicators." *Science* 188 (May 1975):693-99.

Simon, Herbert A. *The New Science of Management Decision*. Rev. ed. Englewood Cliffs, N.J.: Prentice-Hall, 1977.

Smith, Glynton. "Systematic Information Sharing in Participative University Management." *Journal of Higher Education* 51 (September/October 1980):519-26.

BIBLIOGRAPHY

Van Maanen, John, ed. "Reclaiming Qualitative Methods for Organizational Research: A Preface." *Administrative Science Quarterly* 24 (December 1979):520-26.

Warwick, D. "A Transactional Approach to Organizations." Syllabus, A-645. Harvard University, Spring 1979.

Weber, Max. *The Theory of Social and Economic Organization.* Edited by A. M. Henderson and Talcott Parsons. Glencoe, Ill.: Free Press, 1947.

Weisman, Herman M. *Information Systems, Services, and Centers.* New York: Becker and Hayes, 1972.

The NCHEMS
Executive Overview Series

Each year, the NCHEMS Executive Overview subscription will elucidate a general theme. The theme for 1982 is Decisions and Decision Information.

The central problem of sound decisionmaking in higher education is how to arrive at informed, forward-looking decisions—decisions that maximize institutional effectiveness while minimizing the negative impacts of financial stress, shifting program demand, and changing clientele. Established decision processes usually were not intended to cope with a quick succession of decisions involving far-reaching change. Similarly, conventional sources and channels of information often are inadequate to meet today's decision needs.

Each Executive Overview in the 1982 Subscription will explore some key aspects of the administrator's decision responsibility.

The 1982 Executive Overview Subscription includes six books in the series, plus a bonus book for subscribers. The cost is $60, or $70 outside the continental United States.

The books are also available individually at $10.00 each plus 50¢ per copy for shipping and handling.

The 1982 NCHEMS Executive Overview Series:

Data and Information for Executive Decisions in Higher Education By Dennis P. Jones

The Effective Use of Management Consultants in Higher Education By Jana B. Matthews

Decisions and Decision Processes in Higher Education: Theory and Reality By Ellen Earle Chaffee

How to Acquire and Use Student-Outcomes Information By Peter T. Ewell

Program Review in Higher Education: From Within and From Without By Robert J. Barak

Comparative Data in Higher Education By Paul Brinkman and Jack Krakower

Bonus for Subscribers—

A Survival Kit for Invisible Colleges, 2nd ed. By Norbert J. Hruby, President, Aquinas College

Order Form

Six Books in the Series plus a Bonus for Subscribers!

☐ I wish to subscribe to the NCHEMS 1982 Executive Overview Subscription ($60 for one year, $70 for one year outside the continental United States)

Name _____ Title _____

Department _____ Institution _____

Address _____ City _____ State _____ Zip _____

☐ Payment Enclosed
(Please make checks payable to NCHEMS)

☐ Charge Institutional Purchase Order # _____
(Enclose Purchase Order with this form)

☐ I do not wish to subscribe, but I would like to receive the 1982 Executive Overviews listed below at $10.00 each:

QTY.	TITLE	PRICE
____	_____	____
____	_____	____
____	_____	____
____	_____	____
____	_____	____

Plus 50¢ per book for shipping and handling ____

Total ____

RETURN TO:
NCHEMS Publications Department/P.O. Drawer P/Boulder, Colorado 80302
or call (303) 497-0390

59

Order Form

Six Books in the Series plus a Bonus for Subscribers!

☐ I wish to subscribe to the NCHEMS 1982 Executive Overview Subscription ($60 for one year, $70 for one year outside the continental United States)

Name_____ Title_____

Department_____ Institution_____

Address_____ City_____ State_____ Zip_____

☐ Payment Enclosed   ☐ Charge Institutional Purchase Order #_____
(Please make checks payable to NCHEMS)   (Enclose Purchase Order with this form)

☐ I do not wish to subscribe, but I would like to receive the 1982 Executive Overviews listed
below at $10.00 each:

QTY.	TITLE	PRICE

Plus 50¢ per book for shipping and handling _____

Total _____

RETURN TO:
NCHEMS Publications Department / P.O. Drawer P / Boulder, Colorado 80302
or call (303) 497-0390